WE
THE PEOPLE
SQUANTO

Published by Creative Education, Inc.
123 South Broad Street
Mankato, Minnesota 56001
Printed in the United States of
America.

Cataloging in process information is
available upon request from the
publisher.

WE
THE PEOPLE
SQUANTO

THE INDIAN WHO SAVED THE PILGRIMS
(1500(?)-1622)

JAMES R. ROTHAUS

Illustrated By John Nelson And Harold Henriksen

CREATIVE EDUCATION

SQUANTO

Late in the 1500's, a boy named Tisquantum was born in an Indian village named Patuxet. His people belonged to the Wampanoag tribe. They lived in what is now Massachusetts and Rhode Island.

If Tisquantum had been born a few years earlier, surely he would

have lived as his people had lived for thousands of years—hunting game, harvesting corn and beans, and protecting their beloved land from enemy tribes. Instead, the young Indian boy was destined to play an important part in the settlement of America by the first colonists from Europe in the 1600's.

Our story begins in 1603 when Tisquantum was still a very young boy. That year a great English ship captained by Martin Pring sailed to the shores of Tisquantum's village.

Like other explorers before him, Pring was impressed by the friendly Indian people. He saw that the land was big and beautiful. The earth was fertile. The bays and rivers were teeming with fish, and the forests abounded with valuable fur-bearing animals. Tisquantum's tribe had no way of knowing that many other English explorers, fur traders and merchants were already planning to sail to the land of the Indian to make their fortunes.

Two years later, another captain named George Waymouth came to Tisquantum's village. Waymouth did something that changed Tisquantum's life forever. He kidnapped five Indians and brought them back to England with him. Many historians believe that one of these Indians was Tisquantum.

Captain Waymouth treated his captives kindly. He introduced the Indians to people in England in the hopes that Europeans would become

more interested in the New World.

Tisquantum lived in England for eight years. He was given a new name—Squanto—by the white people. In time, Squanto learned to speak English. He marvelled at the huge stone buildings, the fancy horse-drawn carriages, and the peculiar customs of the white Europeans. But always in his heart, the Indian longed to return to his family and friends in Patuxet village.

During this time, ships from many countries explored the New World. Some Englishmen wanted to start colonies there. Like the earlier explorers, they too thought they could make money by sending furs and other goods from Indian lands back to England.

One day Squanto met Captain John Smith, a dashing, good-hearted Englishman who was sailing for America. Captain Smith had a dream. He hoped to start a peaceful, prosperous colony in New England.

When Squanto heard this, his heart raced. "Please, Captain, take me with you," pleaded the Indian boy. "Take me home on your ship, and I promise to find a way to repay your kindness."

Slowly, a big smile spread across John Smith's handsome face. "Maybe you *can* help me," said the Captain as he ruffled Squanto's hair with one big hand. "But if I agree to take you, you must promise to tell the Indians that we are their friends.

I cannot get investors for my colony if the Indians kill settlers."

Squanto agreed. In 1614, two ships sailed for Massachusetts. The captain of one was John Smith. But the other captain was a greedy, scheming man named Thomas Hunt. Trouble lay ahead.

Hunt was jealous of John Smith. He did not want Smith's plan to succeed. During the long voyage to America, Hunt silently hatched an evil plan. When Captain Smith left Squanto at his home village of Patuxet and sailed away to explore, Hunt stayed at Patuxet to put his scheme to work.

True to his promise, Squanto assured the Wampanoag people that Englishmen were good. Some chiefs

said: "Then why did they kidnap you?" Squanto promised them that this would never happen again.

Meanwhile, the evil Hunt watched and waited. When he was sure that Squanto had finally won the trust of the tribe, he lured about 30 Indians onto his ship, with Squanto. The trap was sprung! Hunt had the Indians put in chains. Then he quickly set sail for Spain.

"You Indians will be sold as slaves," he sneered. "That will fix John Smith."

On the long voyage to Spain, poor Squanto felt all the sorrow of the other Indians in his own heart. He was angry and ashamed. In his rush to help the English, he had only betrayed his own people. In

Spain, a few of the Indians were sold as slaves.

Then a miracle occurred. Somehow, a group of Christian monks found out what was happening. They said: "It is wrong to make slaves of these Indians."

Spanish soldiers forced the Englishmen to release the Indians to the monks. Squanto and the others were treated well. After severals years, Squanto was able to go to England.

Now, he was excited again. "When I get to England," he thought, "I can find a way to go home!"

But Squanto returned to an England that was in deep trouble. Many people were hunted by soldiers or even forced to leave the country, simply because they wanted to worship God in their own way.

Some of these persecuted people looked to the New World.

About the time that Squanto returned to England, one religious group had fled to Holland to escape the English King. They, like Squanto, were trying to find a ship that would take them to America. History has given these people the name Pilgrims. In the years to come, Squanto and the Pilgrims would

cross paths in a very special way in America.

In 1619, Squanto finally succeeded in booking passage on a ship bound for home. Captain Thomas Dermer was sailing to Newfoundland and Squanto was invited aboard. His heart overflowed with joy.

They sailed down to Maine, where they met Samoset, a leader of the Abnaki tribe. Friendly Samoset went with Captain Dermer, Squanto, and some Englishmen to Patuxet. There a terrible scene awaited them.

Squanto's home was gone! There had been a terrible sickness. All the Indian people had died. The beautiful village had been burned to stop the sickness. Only ashes remained. Of all the people of Patuxet, Squanto was the only one left alive. Filled with sorrow, Squanto wondered why he alone had been spared. Did the Great Spirit have a plan for his life? If so, what could it be?

Later, Captain Dermer took Squanto and Samoset to visit Massasoit, the Head Chief of all the Wampanoag Indian people. Because Squanto spoke well of the English, Chief Massasoit promised to be a good friend to any colonists who came.

Then Captain Dermer left Squanto and Samoset and sailed away. Meanwhile, back in Europe, Pilgrims had found a ship at last.

On November 21, 1620, 102 colonists landed at Cape Cod.

The Pilgrims explored, then decided to settle at Patuxet, the site of Squanto's old village. They named their new colony "Plymouth" and set about building a better life in America.

Then the winter wind and

snow swept in on them from the frigid Atlantic Ocean. The Pilgrims had a terrible winter, with hunger and sickness. Food and supplies were scarce. About 50 died. The rest worried about their future in the colony.

In March, 1621, Samoset found them. They were amazed when he said, "Welcome!" in the English he had learned from Squanto.

Squanto himself hurried to Plymouth colony as soon as Samoset told him the news. Not far behind was Massasoit and a huge band of warriors.

With Squanto's help, the Pilgrims and the Head Chief of the Wampanoag made a peace treaty.

It was to last more than 50 years. Massasoit and his warriors departed. But Squanto said:

"I am going to stay here with you. I will be a friend and helper to those who will build a new village where my peoples' village once stood."

The Pilgrims had come to the New World knowing nothing of how to make a living there. Squanto had to teach them. Without his help, the little colony and its American dream would have surely perished.

He showed them how to catch fish in the river. They knew nothing about the planting of corn. He showed them how to bury three fish with each seed, which gave the sprouting corn its fertilizer.

He helped them to hunt. They took deer, ducks, wild geese, turkeys, and other game. He showed them which fruits and berries were good, which green plants were fit to eat and which were medicine.

All summer long he worked with them, living in a little house he had built near the river. They became his people—taking the place of the village that had disappeared.

Governor Bradford said of Squanto: "He was a special instrument sent of God." Not only was he a teacher, but also a diplomat. He helped the Colonists to get along with Massasoit and with the people of the nearby Nauset tribe.

In the fall of 1621, the Pilgrims brought in a good harvest.

They invited Massasoit and his men to a three-day feast—the first Thanksgiving. And Squanto was an honored guest.

He stayed with them for another year. In the fall of 1622, Squanto took sick and died while on a trading voyage with the Pilgrims. Sorrowing, they laid their friend to rest near Chatham, Cape Cod.

Today, when Americans look back with pride on the courageous men and women who risked their lives to launch a free country, we remember Squanto—friend, helper, peace-maker and brother.

WE THE PEOPLE SERIES

WOMEN OF AMERICA

CLARA BARTON
JANE ADDAMS
ELIZABETH BLACKWELL
HARRIET TUBMAN
SUSAN B. ANTHONY
DOLLEY MADISON

INDIANS OF AMERICA

GERONIMO
CRAZY HORSE
CHIEF JOSEPH
PONTIAC
SQUANTO
OSCEOLA

FRONTIERSMEN OF AMERICA

DANIEL BOONE
BUFFALO BILL
JIM BRIDGER
FRANCIS MARION
DAVY CROCKETT
KIT CARSON

WAR HEROES OF AMERICA

JOHN PAUL JONES
PAUL REVERE
ROBERT E. LEE
ULYSSES S. GRANT
SAM HOUSTON
LAFAYETTE

EXPLORERS OF AMERICA

COLUMBUS
LEIF ERICSON
DeSOTO
LEWIS AND CLARK
CHAMPLAIN
CORONADO